HOW THE SOUTH
WON THE CIVIL WAR

HOW THE SOUTH WON THE CIVIL WAR

And How It Affects Us Today

Frank R. Barreca

Strategic Book Publishing and Rights Co.

© 2013 by Frank R. Barreca
All rights reserved. First edition 2013.

No part of this book may be reproduced or transmitted in any form or by any means, graphic, electronic, or mechanical, including photocopying, recording, taping, or by any information storage retrieval system, without the permission, in writing, from the publisher.

Strategic Book Publishing and Rights Co.
12620 FM 1960, Suite A4-507
Houston, TX 77065
www.sbpra.com

ISBN: 978-1-62516-104-8

Book Design by Julius Kiskis

21 20 19 18 17 16 15 14 13   1 2 3 4 5

DEDICATION

This book is dedicated to all the citizens of this republic of ours with the hope that we will all wake up to the problems from within that face the very foundations of our great country.

CONTENTS

Acknowledgments ix

Preface xi

The Early Years 1

Basic Facts About the Southern Victory 4

Black Society and Its Leaders 10

Mexican Society and Its Leaders 16

How Terminology Adds to the Problem 19

Unions and Other Minority Groups 23

Journalism and Its Failures Today 29

The US Congress—A New House of Lords? 36

Governing Boards and Educational Institutions—The Root of the Problem? 40

Epilogue: Wake Up America 51

ACKNOWLEDGMENTS

To my wife, Gail, for her continued support and patience in hearing me rehash the incidents described in this book. Her suggestions and editing were invaluable.

PREFACE

The contents and conclusions reached in this book are a result of over eighty years on this planet observing, studying, and researching various aspects of life in this republic of ours. I choose the word "republic" because I have come to believe that most people don't know what it means and use the word "democracy" as a substitute.

I started this book as a result of the fear I have that this country of ours is in danger. This is not a danger from outside sources, but from within. There are people who, either knowingly or unknowingly, are leading us toward a system that moves us away from our constitutional republic. They are leading us toward a socialist system with supreme national power, to the detriment of states' rights and away from the will of the majority of our citizens. Maybe good-sounding words, such as "liberal" or "progressive," are adding to our problem.

Most of the things I write about in this book are drawn from my personal experiences over this rather long lifetime, along with some research I was able to do, quite by accident, during my naval reserve duty, when I was assigned to the Chief of Information's office in the Pentagon, in the Minority Affairs Division.

Some of the thoughts on issues I raise came from conversations with a former congressman from Arizona, the late Morris K. (Mo) Udall. We had the opportunity to talk about many things while we were washing dishes to work our way through school after the war at the University of Arizona in the mid to late '40s. Mo and I didn't agree on a number of issues, with Mo leaning toward liberalism and myself taking a more conservative viewpoint. However, I strongly supported his view then and also while he was a congressman from Arizona that term limits should be established to eliminate the current seniority system in the Congress of the United States of America.

I mention this now since it is basic to issues raised in this book. As I write this, I can see that there will be other items that will step on toes and challenge some old traditions. But I must do it because I believe that this country is in danger of losing the qualities that the founding fathers envisioned for this republic of ours. There are people who, for various reasons, are steering us away from our Constitution and trying to make the national government supreme in everything. Some would like to see us in a new world order—a One World Order. Others are inciting class warfare.

These types of ideas can bring this country down into socialism, which some appear to favor. They support it under other names, which sound good. But these ideas are robbing our country of the energy that made us great. We haven't done everything right. We all make mistakes. But the United States of America has been a haven of freedom and opportunity for people from all over the world. I hope this book, in some small way, will help prevent that from changing.

THE EARLY YEARS

It is my premise that the South did, in effect, win the Civil War, because of the results of events that took place in national and state elections in the fifteen years after that war. Those conditions continued for another sixty-five years, until after World War II. The purpose of this book is to show how these events occurred and how they affect us today.

I was not aware of the racial separatism in this country during my early years of growing up in the '20s, '30s, and early '40s. It was only after I had left home to enter the service in World War II that I realized what was going on. I grew up in the Berkshire Hills of Massachusetts—Pittsfield, to be exact—during the Great Depression. My parents were immigrants, with my mother arriving with her mother at Ellis Island at six months of age in 1895 and my father arriving alone at eighteen years of age in 1910.

I didn't learn to speak Italian in those early, formative years because my parents embraced America totally and with fervor, which was typical of many immigrants of that time. The lesson our family taught us as children was quite simple: "Learn English, study hard, and get an education, for this is the land of opportunity and freedom." And, most importantly, we were not hyphenated Americans, such as Italian-American, Spanish-American, Mexican-American, African-American, or Irish-American. We were Americans and proud of it. That was the only answer we gave when asked about our nationality. This, to me, is one of the items that divide us. It's fine to be proud of your ancestors and where they came from, but our true and only allegiance should be to the United States of America. This background has had a profound influence on my relationship to the race situation.

As I have looked back through the years, I have realized more and more how great and true that lesson was for me and for my two brothers. Eight years separate me from my older brother, because of the childhood death of twins during those intervening years, and only three years separate me from my younger brother.

Growing up during the Depression years is hard for me to remember as being bad. My father had a position that allowed him to work through the Depression—sometimes only two or three days a week, but he always had a job and, therefore, income.

My mother was a beautiful woman who loved music and the arts. As a result there were music lessons, dance lessons, and singing lessons to go along with our academic studies. She also read up on etiquette, and Emily Post was the authority. In this land of opportunity, table manners were important, with the proper placement and use of silverware, glassware, and napkins.

Manners were everything. If we were in a room or on a bus and a woman came in, we were to get up and offer our seat. Of course, contrary to what happens today, when we went indoors, we immediately removed our hats. It was in very bad taste not to do so, especially when sitting down at a table to eat. Obviously, this display of etiquette is not observed by everyone today.

I don't think any of us brothers growing up and going to high school in Pittsfield had any idea of the life of black people in other parts of the country. There were only a few in Pittsfield and they were in class with us and accepted just as any other students would be accepted.

When I entered the navy during World War II at seventeen years of age, I applied for the Naval Aviation Cadet Program, passed the examinations, and was accepted. This was at a time when we were losing many pilots. At the beginning of the war, you had to have four years of college to apply, then the requirement was lowered to two years of college, and, finally, applicants were accepted right out of high school, if they could pass the exams. Almost immediately, my call came to report to the navy's Fargo Building in Boston for processing.

BASIC FACTS ABOUT THE SOUTHERN VICTORY

I first became aware of the fact that the South, in one respect, really won the Civil War during one of my summer naval reserve duties. I usually put in for my summer duties aboard aircraft carriers, ships at sea, or naval air stations. But finally, because of my many years of experience working in newspaper, radio, and television and acquiring an additional designation as a Public Affairs Officer, I applied for reserve duty in the Chief of Information's office in the Pentagon.

I had not heard back about my application for some time, until one day, in my office at the University of Arizona, my secretary popped her head in the door and said, "There's a call for Commander Barreca from the Pentagon." When she said my last name she rolled the Rs.

I answered the phone, without rolling the Rs in my name, since I had never done so, and there was a distinct pause. I think they thought they were calling a naval officer who, in their minds, was a minority. I was told that the admiral did not have any openings on his staff that summer, but I was asked if I would undertake a special assignment in the Minority Affairs Office. The navy was under pressure at the time because of a lack of minority pilots and officers. They wanted to develop materials to attract minority candidates, especially blacks.

I accepted the assignment and reported for duty. As a first step, I decided to research navy records to see if there were any blacks who were or had been in the navy who could serve as role models for the young people of that time.

I chose to start my search with a date right after the end of the Civil War. Don't ask me why I picked that starting point—it was just an arbitrary decision. I asked for and began receiving personnel records of black enlisted men and officers at the rate of about ten to twenty at a time. I was amazed at the number of records and what they showed. There were numerous captains of ships and many recipients of medals for valor in combat.

However, after the year 1875, the number of records delivered for each year dramatically decreased. By 1900, there were very few records of blacks in the navy, and I received a note that by 1910 there were no blacks in the navy.

I had been discussing this situation at lunches with another reservist on summer duty. These discussions prompted me to find out why there suddenly were no blacks in the navy and to check for possible answers. What I found out proved to be very interesting.

Following the defeat by the Union army of the eleven southern states of the Confederacy (Virginia, West Virginia, Kentucky, Tennessee, North Carolina, South Carolina, Georgia, Alabama, Mississippi, Louisiana, and Texas), the United States had a ten-year period called Reconstruction.

It should be noted that President Abraham Lincoln was the head of the Republican Party. When, under his leadership, he delivered his Emancipation Proclamation, there was a proposal in Congress to abolish slavery. The Republicans were the abolitionists.

A cursory study of history shows that as a result of the move to abolish slavery, the eleven southern states decided to break away from the Union and form their own Confederacy. The senators and representatives from those states who were not Democrats became Democrats and then attempted to secede from the United States of America.

Following the defeat by the Union Army of the eleven southern states, the ten-year period called Reconstruction began in 1865.

All the governors of these states were Republicans from the North, appointed by the government and backed by the occupying Union army. This was to make sure that the abolition of slavery was carried out. This, of course, led to the derogatory name "carpetbagger," coined from the luggage of that period carried by the governors who commuted from their homes in the North.

During this time of Reconstruction, the blacks were making progress in moving into American society. Of course, much of this progress was in the North. The year 1875 marked the end of the ten-year Reconstruction progress. In the state elections of that year, every single one of the eleven southern states elected Democrats as their governors. This also was the year that every single southern state passed Jim Crow laws. The Democrats of the South essentially stopped all the gains that blacks had been able to accomplish since the end of the Civil War. The Democrat segregation policy, as expressed in the Jim Crow laws, such as separate drinking fountains, separate restrooms, separate schools—and the list goes on and on—was blatant discrimination against the very people for whom the war was fought.

This terrible injustice continued for about seventy-five years, until after World War II. Some people might ask, "How could this continue for so long?" The answer probably is that politics played a key role. The southern Democrats stuck together during those years, voting as a bloc. To get anything done, those from other parts of the country apparently went along with it. In other words, they compromised.

Woodrow Wilson became president near the beginning of the 20th century. President Wilson was born in 1858. He was elected president in 1913. He was the leader of the "Progressive" movement. He brought many of the southern Democrats into the White House and started the enforcement of segregation in many federal offices. His earlier speeches and writings were very racist and derogatory about blacks and their roles in our society.

For example, he had said, "Segregation is not a humiliation but a benefit and ought to be so regarded." While a member of the Ku Klux Klan, he wrote that the purpose of segregation was "To attempt by intimidation what they were not able to attempt by the ballot or by an ordered course of public action."

While he was President of Princeton University, prior to his election as President of the United States, he discouraged blacks from even applying for admission. As President of the United States, he did not interfere with the established Jim Crow laws, which were enacted in 1875. He backed demands of southern Democrats who said that states should be left alone to deal with issues of race and black voting. One among his many racist actions was when his administration adopted segregation policies that eliminated blacks from the military. All of this continued up until World War II.

Through the years leading up to World War II, many colorful Democrats acted openly racist and maintained a bloc in Congress that kept the Jim Crow laws in effect.

During these years, prominent Democrat politicians were known for their racist speeches and writings that dealt with the Jim Crow laws and "keeping Negroes in their place."

In more recent times, there was Harry Byrd, a Democrat representative and then senator from West Virginia. Why didn't black religious and political leaders speak out against this racist man? Senator Byrd voted against the Civil Rights Act of 1961.

He defended the Ku Klux Klan during his campaign during the 1950s when he was forty-one years old. He even used the phrase "White N*****" on a national television broadcast. In 1946 Harry Byrd wrote, "The Klan is needed today more than ever before and I am anxious to see it back here in Virginia."

Despite Senator Byrd's record of racism, the National Association for the Advancement of Colored People (NAACP) gave him a 100 percent rating during the 108th Congress. Where were the religious and political leaders of the black community at that time? Were they beholden to the Democrat Party to keep their positions of power and income? Incidentally, Senator Byrd, who had been a Democrat from his start in politics, changed his party affiliation in later years when his reelection seemed in doubt.

During Franklin Delano Roosevelt's administration, a period of which Democrats are very proud, the most powerful man in government was a known racist representing only 1,500 people from Uvalde, Texas, John Nance Garner. He had been the 44th Speaker of the House of Representatives and in 1933 became the nation's 32nd Vice President under President Roosevelt.

His speeches and writings were as racist as could be. Yet because of the congressional seniority system, this man, representing only a minute percentage of the nation's population, could continue to spearhead suppression of blacks in this country.

If this discrimination, led by Democrats, had not happened, and if there had been a gradual period of integration and education during those seventy-five years, as there had been during the ten-year Republican Reconstruction period following the Civil War, we wouldn't have needed the race riots that ensued to finally bring about the equality and justice that was long overdue.

How can blacks be so loyal to the political party that opposed their freedom and equality along with the rest of the American population? Surely their religious and political leaders should have been aware of these historical facts. Haven't they known the difference between friend and foe? Or has money, prestige, and power had an influence on them? Unfortunately, it appears that their leaders do not appear to be interested in anything but remaining as leaders to protect their political and religious positions and the resulting income.

The above explains why I maintain that the South did, in effect, win the Civil War. How the southern Democrats approached politics after the Reconstruction period has affected many of the things occurring in our society today. But another important question remains. Do the leaders of the black community, who should know the history of the Democrat Party, put their own personal, political, and financial interests above those of their constituents? Are they really helping all their people enter the mainstream of American society?

BLACK SOCIETY AND ITS LEADERS

Since the end of Reconstruction in 1875, black society, due to the segregationist policies instituted by the Democrats, particularly in the South, made very little progress in its integration into the general population. It was difficult for black society to do so as well as politically impossible, since it had no power. With the advent of World War II and the exposure of many young blacks to opportunities they never would have had previously, the desire for equality under the law became paramount.

Martin Luther King Jr. emerged as their leader, and, finally, equality under the law became a reality. But they faced three basic problems—education, politics, and religious leadership.

You could say that the black community, as a whole, was now facing the same problem that every immigrant to this country has faced: integration into an American society that was already here and firmly established.

The immigrants had to face discrimination in getting jobs, finding places to live, and learning a new language. But they came in droves from various countries, mostly for the same reasons—"freedom" and "opportunity." They had heard about this land called America, where there was the freedom to work and worship and live in a democratic society. Most had suffered privation or oppression from totalitarian societies. This was the land where, if you worked hard, learned English, and got an education, you had the opportunity to go as far as your mind and body could carry you.

When I was growing up, sports were a way of getting a college education. So while immigrant parents worked hard to support their families, their male children went into sports with a vengeance. The college teams of my boyhood were filled with athletes with Polish names, Irish names, German names, and Italian names. They played their sports, but they also studied hard. In one generation, they became the nation's lawyers, doctors, engineers, teachers, and accountants and moved into a different level of American life.

The biggest migrations into the country began in around the 1830s with the Germans, when their lands in Europe played out after centuries of farming without the benefit of modern-day fertilizers. German immigrants suffered discrimination from the people who were already in this country. The Germans were newcomers who were all vying for the same jobs. Then, in about 1845, the Irish began to come over and meet the same kinds of problems. In around 1880 Italian immigration began and the Irish became their competitors.

In recent times, we have had the "N-word" thrown at blacks. When I was growing up, I had many fights when the "wop" and "guinea" slurs were thrown at those of us whose parents had come from Italy. The word "wop" came from Ellis Island, where many immigrants would be tagged with it, and meant "without papers." There were similar derogatory names for other immigrants, such as Krauts and Polacks.

Today, however, sports are more often looked at as a way to big money rather than an education. How many times have you seen student athletes sign up with a college and in one or two years leave for the professional teams? And from personal experience, I can tell you that too many of them have had little or no education.

A long time—over thirty years—ago, I retired from the University of Arizona. I remember discussing this situation with the dean of students. We thought, humorously, that we had a good solution to the problem. Since university teams have virtually turned into farm clubs for the professional teams, colleges and universities should get together and negotiate with the pros to fund the collegiate farm teams and pay the players a stipend. Those who want an education will take classes, tuition-free, with a stipulation that each athlete will spend at least three years in college. The others can play their sports and hope to make the professional teams. Obviously, I don't think anyone will go for this plan today.

Although it has been over fifty years since the civil rights laws were enacted, I don't believe that blacks, to a great extent, have taken full advantage of all the opportunities available to them, except for in the entertainment industry and sports. When an individual black person achieves success on his or her own, many times he or she is labeled an "Uncle Tom" or an "Aunt Jemima." In fact, if a black person was a Republican and successful, it could be even worse.

This was the case in the appointment by a Republican president of Clarence Thomas to the Supreme Court. There didn't seem to be an appreciation for what this black lawyer had achieved. Was it because a Republican had made the appointment, or that Clarence Thomas earned it without the help of the traditional black leadership? And, of course, you had some black senators voting against his appointment, including forty-six of the fifty-seven Democrats.

Comedian Bill Cosby, who had achieved fame in both film and television and earned a PhD in education, criticized his people for not bringing up their children properly. He talked about the foul language in "gangsta" rap, involvement in drugs, high school dropouts, and the high crime rate. He admonished them to do better in how they lived and brought up their children. Immediately he was criticized and labeled an "Uncle Tom."

Unfortunately, what you have are black political and religious leaders constantly preaching how bad things are, how bad they have been treated, and how the world owes them a living. So, instead of doing what every other immigrant group did—tell their children to work hard, learn English, and get a good education—they continually tell them how bad things are for them, causing a lack of incentive for young people to compete in modern-day society. This defeatist attitude is prominently displayed and preached by many of these political and religious leaders.

A number of people might find fault with the following, but I believe that what has hurt black progress the most over the past fifty years has not been white racism, but rather the black leadership. In this regard, I am referring to some political and religious leaders throughout the country on both the national and local scenes.

They have constantly preached to their people how bad things are for them and how badly they need these leaders to help them get ahead. When you hear this kind of propaganda in school and in church for so many years, you begin to believe it. Therefore, for many, there is little incentive to better one's self and get ahead. What they hear from these so-called leaders is: It's hopeless, and so why try to get ahead? At the same time, they ask for votes and financial support so they can continue their careers.

The leaders, on their part, have an incentive to keep this kind of mind-set because it's their livelihood. Much of their income is derived from these followers who believe that the country is still racist. I thought that idea would have been dispelled with the last two presidential elections.

If whites were so racist, how could a man of color have been elected to the Office of President? Without the white vote, this president would not have been elected. There should be a push on the part of these leaders to get their people educated and into the mainstream of American life. Most Americans would welcome and applaud this change in attitude.

Black people who have excelled in their fields are appreciated by most white people. They honor those who have achieved success, as you have seen, in music, theater, education, law, medicine, sports, and the list goes on. But I do believe that many are getting tired of black leaders crying "racism" whenever criticism is leveled at a black person.

Just look at the situation three blacks found themselves in recently. I am talking about Congressman Charles Rangel, Rev. Al Sharpton, and Congresswoman Maxine Waters. They are defiant in defending themselves against charges of wrongdoing, and the least bit of criticism against them is cited as racist. It's nothing of the sort. Through the years, whites have been accused of similar violations of the law and criticisms of them have not been considered racist. Why the difference now? This is what the leaders have been telling their followers, so why stop now? It's a convenient crutch.

If the role of the Democrat Party in racism before the Civil War and afterward was properly taught in schools, would blacks still register in such great numbers in the Democrat Party? This is the party that has done them in for over 150 years! From what I know of the real history of race relations in this country, if I were an educated black man, I would be embarrassed to be a member of the Democrat Party.

But minority groups are not strangers to the Democrat Party. The party succeeds for that very reason. The party seeks these blocs of voters who will stick together at election times. Some of the obvious groups, in addition to blacks, who are members and supporters of the Democrat Party are: unions and guilds of all kinds, the American Civil Liberties Union, abortion supporters, and homosexuals, just to name a few.

What this produces, in many cases, is victory for minority viewpoints because various leaders will try to carry the day for its member groups. As a result, you have a violation of one of our principles that the majority rules. We have many cases of the will of the majority of the people being subordinated to the wishes of diverse, smaller groups who find success moving their proposals forward in the Democrat Party.

MEXICAN SOCIETY AND ITS LEADERS

I should point out that the situation I described in the previous chapter is also true for another group—those people who have come from south of our border with Mexico.

Their situation is a little different since there was no slavery in their history in this country. But, as I mentioned before, most have immigrated into this country for a better life in what they have heard of as a democracy. And, of course, they have been told of our democracy and so they wind up as Democrats. This is especially true in the American border states.

Far too many know little or no English when they first arrive so they rely on the help and advice of those already here who speak their native language. This is where those interested in politics get involved. As soon as they become citizens they are encouraged to register and vote Democrat, which provides a solid bloc of votes at election time.

Why do you think Democrat politicians in Washington and locally in the Southwest are pushing for complete amnesty for all the illegal immigrants who are already here? They promote it as compassion and the right thing to do. Obviously, they see this as millions of new votes to count for the Democrat Party. This is not the kind of America that the founding fathers envisioned.

As I revisit this chapter many months later, there is new support for what I have written above. A few years back, President Obama said that he was powerless, legally, to do anything about the status of illegal immigrants in this country. But with an election coming up, he bypassed the Congress of the United States and unilaterally stopped deportation of some illegal immigrants. Can anyone say this is not a move to gain votes from a particular group of people?

Another indication that something is terribly wrong is what has happened in an Arizona school district. First of all, I should remind you that I am totally against the use of the hyphen in describing our nationality. We are Americans with no allegiance to any other country. I believe the hyphen, such as in Italian-American, Irish-American, and Mexican-American, tends to divide us. We shouldn't be labeling ourselves with where our ancestors originated. As far as I am concerned, the use of the hyphen only serves to divide us.

Unfortunately, a school district in Tucson, Arizona, had an ethnic studies course that served to divide us even more. It was ruled in violation of the law by an administrative law judge, and the state superintendent of education threatened to take away fourteen million dollars from the district if it was not stopped.

Among the facts that the students were taught are the following: "The southwestern area of the United States of America was stolen from Mexico and should be given back to Mexico." "They should be proud to be Mexicans and speak the language of Mexico." One of our congressmen has been recorded telling a student how proud he was of this student as a Mexican and how well the student spoke the language of Mexico. In my opinion, we should be encouraging students to learn and speak English, the language of this country.

The main complaint was that this program was racist in setting one race against another. In fact, this La Raza studies program was nothing more than a lesson in Marxism.

Why were these students not being encouraged to speak

English and to be good Americans? Furthermore, the land was not stolen. If you ask educated people in the northern part of Mexico about this issue, they laugh when they hear about those statements north of the border. They point out that the people in Mexico City at the time of the purchase were happy to get those millions of dollars, which were paid in the purchase. To the people farther south, the northern border area was of no interest to them and never had been.

I know there is concern about the children of illegal immigrants in this country, but those are concerns that should be addressed by the elected representatives of all of the people. This is a constitutional government and this is a constitutional matter. These types of decisions and laws should be decided by the representatives of all of our citizens and not by the edict of the president. This is what happens in socialist and totalitarian (dictatorial) countries where the people have no say and the power is in the hands of the head of that central government. History shows that this is how Hitler, Mussolini, and Stalin came to power.

HOW TERMINOLOGY ADDS TO THE PROBLEM

Terminology has a big influence on how people respond to the things around them, and especially on the newly arrived immigrants to our country. They may have fled oppression and are seeking freedom from that oppression or are seeking an opportunity to work and earn a living. They have heard about jobs, democracy, and freedom, and this is what they hope to find here. Many came and still come for the opportunities they have heard this country offers to all its citizens.

Unfortunately, they have not heard the word "republic." You know—when you pledge allegiance to our flag and "the republic for which it stands." The founding fathers, in putting together the Declaration of Independence and then the Constitution, by which this country is supposed to operate, did not want a pure democracy where the people have supreme power and every citizen gets to vote on every issue. Instead, they founded a republic where the people exert their democratic power through elected representatives who must follow the mandates of the Constitution.

The following are some definitions that may help to illustrate the differences[1]:

democracy—a noun, describing a government in which the supreme power is held by the people.

Webster's New Explorer Large Print Dictionary – New Edition

republic — a noun, describing a government with a representative form of government observing the will of the people.

democrat — a noun, describing a political party, or an adherent of that party.

republican — a noun, describing a political party, or an adherent of that party.

democratic — an adjective, describing actions or beliefs in support of the principle that the power is held by the people in a representative form of government.

With the worldwide publicity of a democracy in the Americas, what did many immigrants do after becoming citizens? They registered and still register in the Democrat Party. You notice I didn't write "Democratic Party," as too many people mistakenly do. I know that many Republicans are just as democratic as Democrats in their actions.

I'll give you a case in point. As I wrote earlier, my father came to this country at eighteen years of age in 1910. Ordinarily, he might not have ever come, since his father was the mayor of the town and they had a retail store in town and a large farm outside of town where hired hands tilled the soil. By the time my father was a young boy, the land had played out and there was no income in the town. To make matters worse, a flash flood in the mountains wiped all the topsoil from the farm.

I still have my father's sea chest at home, in which he carried all his belongings five thousand miles to New York City. In order to get ahead in this new country as fast as he could, he went to a YMCA to get a room so he could learn English and hear it spoken every day. I am told that this was quite unusual, since most Catholics didn't go to Protestant organizations in those years.

I'm not sure how or why he arrived in Pittsfield, Massachusetts, where I grew up. Maybe it was for an opportunity to work, since a GE plant was and still is located there. In any case, as a young man he applied for a job opening and I am told there were twenty-five to thirty applicants in line for that one position, which was to sweep floors. I don't know what he did to impress them, but he got the job.

I don't know how long he stayed in that job, but I do know that when I was growing up in the 1930s—when I was between five and fifteen years of age—my father went to work each day wearing a shirt, tie, and jacket, and he was in charge of the high-voltage testing for the large transformers that were going to the Hoover Dam in Nevada and to a project in the Ural Mountains of Russia.

Politically, he was a registered Democrat. What else would he do? He had achieved his dreams in this "democracy" of the Americas and he became a Democrat. I do remember, however, that this did not last forever. I came home one evening and announced at dinner how much money I had made distributing leaflets in the late afternoon. My father asked where and I told him that it was at the main gate of GE. He didn't use that gate and therefore had not seen me.

When he saw a copy of the leaflet, he was quite dismayed. They were leaflets urging GE employees to join the electrical union. Later, I can remember him coming home from work quite discouraged. The gist of it was that he used to be able to get work done and errors corrected immediately when they occurred. Now he had to talk to the shop steward, who would then decide if a worker was at fault and what needed to be done. It was taking him much longer to get work done compared to the time before the union. It didn't take him very long to shift allegiances and switch to the Republican Party.

I also remember in those years my older brother collecting

newspaper and magazine editorial cartoons. Most of them dealt with such things as unions, communism, liberalism, and progressive subjects. I do remember that they were for a class he was taking in college, which was nearby in Amherst at the University of Massachusetts.

Apparently, progressive and liberal attitudes were being pushed or preached at the college level. How could words like "progressive" or "liberal" be anything but good? World War II then intervened and those two words were not as popular as they had been. I did not notice a resurgence of these two words during my college years immediately following the end of World War II.

But, unfortunately, too many people in the media and in the Democrat Party do not understand the difference in the use of a noun and an adjective with respect to "Democrat" and "democratic."

People are using the adjective "democratic" to identify a member of the Democrat Party. Instead of the adjective, they should be using the noun, and there is a good reason for this. A Republican can be just as democratic in his or her actions as a Democrat. Or, to carry this one step further, a Democrat candidate may not be as democratic in his or her actions as a Republican. Therefore, if you are identifying a member of that party, he or she is not a democratic candidate, but rather a Democrat candidate.

Apparently, from what I read in newspapers and hear and see on radio and television, this distinction and correct usage is not taught in many schools today, especially at the college and university levels.

UNIONS AND OTHER MINORITY GROUPS

What I now write about unions should not be misconstrued. Union membership today accounts for less than 17 percent of our total population. In that small percentage are many good, hardworking people. What they don't realize, however, is what their leaders have done to many parts of the country and how their funds are being used.

Granted, the early sweatshop conditions at the start of the industrial revolution caused many workers to band together for better working conditions and pay. I believe that most objective people today would say that things now have gone too far to the other side. The high wages garnered by this small percentage of the population has resulted in much higher costs for the rest of our population and the loss of many businesses and their suppliers.

The automobile industry is a good example. Today, with the combination of wages and benefits, the cost to a company is about $80 per hour, per employee, which, in one year, costs the company over $166,400 per employee. Hard to believe, isn't it? Let's look at a little history on the effects of unionization.

When I was growing up, New England was the hub of the shoe and textile industries. Shoes, shirts, and other clothing came from New England. As the workers unionized and bargained for higher and higher wages and better benefits, the companies found it harder and harder to earn profits, which would enable them to pay dividends to their investors who created the jobs.

In desperation, these companies moved to the southern states where the unions had not yet made inroads and where labor costs were less. Again, the unions started organizing and wages again began escalating to unreasonable levels.

I think most people know what happened next. The plants moved overseas where costs obviously were much lower. Just look at the labels on men's shirts. They all come from the Far East. Look at the inroads foreign car sales have made versus United States manufacturers. Their hourly costs are half of what US companies have to contend with.

Even the cost of imported goods is affected by unionization at our ports of entry. The following is a good example of where your money goes. A football player from a prominent university ends his eligibility and doesn't graduate from school but is earning over six figures in wages as a longshoreman on the West Coast. Multiply that by the number of dockworkers needed at these ports and you get another view of why your costs are going up. Remember, this is less than 17 percent of the population earning these out-of-kilter wages.

The question then becomes, how do these wages get so high? The answer is complicated but deserves attention. No owner of a company can stand long work stoppages and survive. As a result, the threat of strikes keeps costs going up and up, with no regard to how it affects the other 83 percent of the population. How does this continue? Well, let's go to arbitration. I remember having a number of talks with my younger brother about this arbitration business.

My younger brother is a lawyer, a former chairman of the Board of Trustees of Boston University, and a retired former Vice President of GE, where he handled union negotiations, or arbitration.

Every time a contract governing wages and benefits is about

UNIONS AND OTHER MINORITY GROUPS   25

to expire, both sides come together with their demands. For example, the union representatives come in with their demands for the new contract. Let's say they want a 20 percent increase in wages and benefits even though the cost of living is only going up from 2 to 4 percent. At the current $80-an-hour average in the automobile business, that would raise the average hourly pay and benefits to $96. You can see how wages can and did quickly escalate with this going on every three or five years, depending on the length of the contract.

Meanwhile, the company lawyers come in with their figure of, say, six percent. They then haggle over all the items in the contract while holed up in a hotel in New York for four to eight weeks, and come out with a figure midway between the two extremes, or 13 percent. Now the union lawyers and leaders are happy because they can show their membership what they have done for them. The company now knows what its labor costs are going to be for the next three to five years and can set the price of its products knowing exactly what its labor costs are going to be, without any interruptions. Both parties know from the start that they are going to agree on an increase somewhere between the two figures and it will have no relationship to the cost of living experienced by the rest of the country.

The company also knows that if problems do come up with labor, their supervisors or managers can tell the employee to see their shop steward. It's a cozy arrangement, which only affects the cost of the product you buy. Does anyone really believe that the average worker at GM or Ford is worth $80 per hour? Ask the young people entering the job market at much lower wages.

Added to this problem is the lack of control a company has over its workers. I heard, firsthand, an employee bragging to a group I was in that he only went in to work three days a week. Somebody else signed him in for the other two days. In addition, he pointed out that it only took him four hours to get his work done on each of those three days.

Add to this the power that a strong union has over the life or death of a company. Many have ceased to exist when union demands became too exorbitant. Remember Braniff International Airways? It went out of business because of a strike by the pilots and machinists. The only people who lost money were the investors who helped create the company and the jobs.

Through the years, starting in the early 1900s, the unions have had a strong influence in politics and have always had a strong alliance with the Democrat Party. Their large financial investments in candidates for political office and in issues dealing with union activities have given them great power in the political arena. You have to remember that it is not your average union member who is deeply involved in political issues, but rather the leaders of the movement.

Funds from the members are used to push political agendas favored by the union leaders but not necessarily by all of their members. The unions are just one of the many minority organizations that have found a home in the Democrat Party. The movements within the party have had various labels through the years designed to be saleable to the general American public.

In the early 1900s when being liberal was not as fashionable as it used to be, the word "progressive" was adopted. Who could argue that being progressive wasn't good? Then later being liberal was again deemed to be good. You have an open mind—you're open to new ideas—can that be bad?

In addition to the unions exerting great power in the Democrat Party, you have other groups of people under various banners. You have environmentalists—people who are affecting, adversely, many parts of our economy.

Then you have the groups that advocate for marriages

between males and between females. And then you have those who don't want any cutting of timber in our forests. Two of the groups most seriously affecting our way of life today are those who don't want to drill for oil or mine for coal.

Individually, most of the ideas being pushed by these groups may be opposed by a majority of our citizens. But because these groups, for the most part, belong to and financially support one political party—Democrat—the politicians in that party obviously try to support their constituents, mainly for reelection in the future.

We could have a partial solution to this problem by going back to the proposal made many years ago by a Democrat representative, Morris Udall. The legislation he tried to pass would limit time in office to two consecutive terms. Then Congress could start acting for and listening to the majority of this country's citizens. Of course, this bill was voted down and Congressman Udall lost whatever power he might have had with his colleagues.

At the present time, some of these politicians are working in their own self-interest, which for some is a lifetime career in the Senate or in the House of Representatives.

Many voters do not realize how senators and representatives, through the years, have endowed themselves with all kinds of benefits at the expense of the taxpayers of this country. For example, three years ago they took an automatic increase in their pay when the current financial crisis was beginning. It was at a time when there was no cost of living increase for many people and there was no cost of living increase in pay for social security recipients or most other citizens in the country. I don't even remember the news media informing the public when this occurred, or about later raises.

Individually, most of these are issues opposed by a majority of the population. But because the groups belong to and support the Democrat Party, which tries to please all of its constituents, we have gotten to a point where the minority is overriding the wishes of the majority.

Just look at some of the legislation passed in the last few years. The country is getting to the point where the majority is becoming subordinate to the minority.

This brings up the obvious question of why our senators and representatives go along with this situation. One reason is that the members of our Congress are continually in election mode. Many politicians are hoping for a lifetime career in a political office.

JOURNALISM AND ITS FAILURES TODAY

You may ask, "Why do all of these problems continue?" I believe they continue because of a population that is not well informed and because of people who make a career of continually running for public office. My experiences and thinking lead to this conclusion.

I feel I am in a position to comment on this subject since I spent a good portion of my working life in some form of journalism. I am critical of many of the men and women in all forms of journalism today. I say this because of the way I was introduced to journalism, as a career, over sixty-five years ago.

I had left the navy after the war in December of 1945 because I didn't think there was much of a future for an officer and pilot with only a high school diploma.

The blizzards of December 1945 and January 1946 in the Berkshire Hills of Massachusetts convinced me I needed to get back to a warmer climate. To make a long story short, I wound up at the University of Arizona in Tucson.

Since I had no set idea of what I wanted to do, I registered in the liberal arts department and wound up with a BA degree, with a major in English and a minor in journalism, political science, and economics. I later acquired a master's degree in educational psychology.

The new head of the Department of Journalism was a man by the name of Douglas D Martin. It was the best experience and training I could ever have had. He had been the editor of the *Detroit Free Press* and had won a Pulitzer Prize for his paper's coverage of crime and politics in Chicago. He had just left the paper to come to Arizona for his or his wife's health. To my knowledge, I don't believe he had a PhD. He was hired based on his work experience.

He was adamant about such things as fairness and balance in reporting and simple, clear, concise English in our writing. He was a no-nonsense teacher who treated us as employees—do the work and you get paid with a good grade; don't do the work and you don't get paid and you fail. I have tried to live and work by those standards ever since.

When I graduated in January of 1949, jobs were hard to find. Through a lucky referral, I wound up at a weekly newspaper and printing plant in southern Utah where I served as a reporter and later editor. I then moved to the local radio station as news director. After two years, I returned to Tucson for my wife's health, where I became the news director of KVOA radio. In 1952, when the freeze was lifted on building television stations, I, along with the chief announcer, was assigned to prepare the new television station to go on the air.

I was news director at KVOA-TV for three years, appearing twice nightly doing the on-air broadcasting. One of the things I remember with pride is that I did what Doug Martin had taught us to do. The news was fair, objective, and balanced. As a result, my Democrat friends thought I was a Democrat and my Republican friends thought I was a Republican and I was neither during those years.

In 1955 our station was being sold and I thought it might be a good time to move to a station in San Diego where I could get in more flight time in the naval reserve than I was able to from Tucson. However, that was not to be. I received a call from the

President of the University of Arizona, who had heard about my possible move. He was interested in the new, noncommercial broadcasting and what it might do for education. He was looking for someone who had television experience and made me an offer I couldn't refuse.

I spent the next twenty-five years at the university putting the educational TV and AM and FM (KUAT-TV-AM-FM) stations on the air and serving as general manager. I also was the director of a division called the Radio-TV-Film Bureau. This bureau included the broadcast stations, the closed-circuit installations in various buildings on campus, and the translator stations, which were feeding remote locations around the state with educational courses being taught on television.

Additionally, I and my staff had faculty status in the speech and journalism departments teaching radio, television, and film classes. Our enrollments were increasing so rapidly that I was asked to put together a proposal for a new department. It was called Radio, TV, and Film. As a result I acquired the additional titles of professor and department head.

I also was active on the national, noncommercial broadcasting scene and was elected to the first five-member board of directors in 1969, when we formed the Public Broadcasting Service (PBS). I was reelected twice to serve three terms.

So with that background I am very critical of some of the print and broadcast news as it is practiced today. In my department, we still had some cross-listed courses in speech and journalism, where students from my department would go for such classes as beginning reporting and announcing. I think this is the point where journalism began to change.

I had a couple of students who were talking to me one day about their class in the journalism department. They reported that instead of the fairness and balance that my faculty was emphasizing, the journalism department was pushing what they called "adversarial journalism."

As a result, after over fifty years of this type of teaching, we have many people in the news business giving personal opinions and sharing their personal feelings about a subject, rather than giving a straight reporting of the news in a fair, unbiased manner. Commentary, or editorial opinion, used to be confined to the editorial page(s) or to clearly titled programs in broadcasting. Today you have editorial opinions, or commentary, on the front page, many times with a picture and the name of the reporter. In broadcasting, many reporters pronounce their own feelings about the news as if they were the facts.

Even the comic pages are not free of this. Garry Trudeau's *Doonesbury* strip hardly went a day without making some sort of attack on President George Bush. To me, that strip belonged on the editorial page. That strip today is still an editorial in cartoon format and obviously anti-conservative. It should be obvious to anyone that this strip belongs on the editorial page and not with the rest of the cartoon strips.

Most people have probably heard the charges about the press from the right of the political spectrum and just dismiss them as unproven. One of the schools often mentioned in this vein is Harvard University. During one of President George Bush's campaigns, a noted scholar at Harvard proudly announced to the world that he had taken a survey of the vaunted Harvard faculty and not a single one would vote for President Bush. Can you honestly say that the students at Harvard were or are now getting an unbiased education? How could journalists ignore this pronouncement? It just begged for a follow-up story. But most media ignored the event. They apparently didn't see how it might affect teaching at all.

I tend to believe that journalists have been affected by what some call the "liberal schools" of today. How else can you explain the comment of a prominent reporter of a major television network during an event in a previous presidential campaign? While waiting for the then-candidate, Barack Obama, to enter the room, he said on-air that he had a tingly feeling running up and down his leg when the candidate came into the room. Still, today, I find it hard to believe that any reporter would say such a thing on the air. How fair and balanced can that reporter be in reporting the news?

Let us consider how our journalists covered the campaign of Gov. Sarah Palin, the governor of one of our fifty states, and President Barack Obama, who, at that time, was a first-term senator. I don't know why the news media went after Governor Palin with such a vengeance, unless they wanted to make sure who won the election.

A horde of journalists from all types of media converged on Alaska to see what they could dig up on Governor Palin. If you look back, you will see that many failed to call her Governor but rather just Sarah Palin.

On the other hand, the Democrat candidate received a free ride. Here was a bright, articulate young man, but no one knew much about his background. They didn't dig into his background. There was little mention or investigation of how he could attend a church for twenty-two years without hearing the minister's sermons damning America. And, there was little or no coverage of his relationship with a number of what I would call "unsavory characters."

What was his connection with Bill Ayers, a man who bombed a government building in his early years? Is there any connection between President Obama and George Soros, a big financial supporter of the Democrat Party? Why didn't the press check into the candidate's background? Was his only business experience as a community organizer in Chicago? This lack of investigative reporting stands in stark contrast to what the press did when Governor Palin's candidacy was announced.

Maybe they were afraid of being called racist for attacking the Democrat candidate for the presidency. But I am more prone to judge that they were following the idea of "adversarial journalism," where you choose your foes and your personal opinion interferes with fair and balanced coverage of the news.

As a result, the American public saw an articulate, good-looking young man who eloquently promised "change" that would make everything right with the country. I think that the election results showed, more than anything, that whites are not racist. Without the white vote, President Obama never could have been elected to the office of president.

On the other hand, during President Bush's tenure, many reporters in the radio, television, and print media took delight in making fun of the president. His pronunciation of the word "nuclear" is a good example. He would say "nucular" instead of "nuclear," but I have heard many reporters make the same mistake today. I hear it on radio, television, and cable, even by some well-known journalists. This mispronunciation was supposed to imply that President Bush wasn't too smart.

Why was there little or no news coverage when President Obama referred to the "Corpse" of Engineers instead of using the correct pronunciation of "core"? In the next sentence or two, the president again gave the same incorrect pronunciation. Would our president also be calling one of our military establishments the Marine "Corpse"?

Getting back to President Bush, for the edification of some journalists, anyone who can pass the tests to become an air force fighter pilot is not dumb, as many reporters were inferring. Many reporters didn't even refer to him as President. It was just

"Bush this" and "Bush that." Again, this to me is reflective of "adversarial journalism."

Unfortunately, this situation was not confined to just the journalists. The nighttime network comedians had a field day. It seemed as if almost nightly there were jokes about President Bush but rarely was the title of President used. There was little or no respect for the title of the office. Since that election, you see very little of this type of treatment with reference to the current president.

THE US CONGRESS—A NEW HOUSE OF LORDS?

As I wrote at the beginning of the previous chapter, one of our major problems concerns politicians, many of whom make a career of continually running for office. And when I say continually, I mean from the time they are elected until the next election. Virtually everything they do is judged by the effect it will have on their reelection, not necessarily what is best for the country.

Our founding fathers never intended our Congress to become the counterpart to the British House of Lords. We had a revolution to get away from that tyranny. Our senators and representatives are making careers out of what started out as a short volunteer service, with very little pay, representing the views of their constituency. Over a long period of time, they have become part of the Washington scene and have lost the knowledge of what's really going on back home, except as to how it might affect their reelections.

During 2011, Congress received one of the lowest approval ratings of any Congress. In general, most of our citizens feel that our senators and representatives are not doing a very good job. In fact, Congress is rated the lowest of any part of our political system.

At the time when President Obama was assuming office, the economic situation in the country was getting very bad. The Freddie Mac and Fannie Mae fiascos, overseen by two Democrats,

Congressman Barney Frank and Senator Christopher Dodd, were being severely felt in the housing and construction industries. Many people were losing jobs and homes and therefore income was going down dramatically. At the beginning of that year, our senators and representatives, as I have mentioned earlier, received an automatic pay raise to their already generous pay and benefits.

They accepted this increase as a right rather than considering their job performance and the current economic conditions, which were deteriorating rapidly. This was an automatic raise of $4,100 for each member, bringing their annual salary to $174,000.

These raises, based on the Ethics Reform Act of 1989, happen automatically each year with no debate and no vote. It's automatic unless Congress passes legislation to the contrary. Incidentally, that pay raise for that year cost you, the taxpayers, 2.5 million dollars. Congress has had additional annual raises since 2009 and I have not heard of a time when they have refused these raises when the country has been experiencing dire financial problems.

Now you know why, in a previous chapter, I wrote that we needed to change the system and limit our members of Congress to two consecutive terms.

In their zeal to acquire campaign funds for reelection, our elected representatives do not always vote for what is best for the taxpaying people they represent. Their vote, in too many cases, goes to the individuals or groups that are making the largest campaign contributions. Politicians can blame themselves for the bad image they have in the eyes of the voters.

They are anxious to get "earmarks" for their district or state to strengthen their dreams of reelection. Also, they have increased their salaries at times when conditions did not warrant those increases. When most people were beginning to feel the effects of the growing downturn in our economy, including the real estate crash, both houses of Congress accepted automatic increases in their salaries.

Wouldn't you think that they would have voted in January of 2009 to forgo those increases in view of what was happening to most other American citizens?

This American House of Lords has allowed the expense of government to escalate dramatically. The number of federal employees has grown out of proportion to what the country can afford. An average increase of 450,000 new employees per year is more than taxpayers can afford. The size of the federal government has ballooned out of proportion to the rest of the country in terms of numbers and salaries. If it was important many years ago to limit the President of the United States to two consecutive terms in office, it now becomes even more necessary to limit the terms of our senators and representatives to two consecutive terms in office.

One of the most glaring examples of a dysfunctional Congress was when the Senate passed the Patient Protection and Affordable Care Act, commonly called "Obamacare." Here was a bill thousands of pages long and the leader of the House, Democrat Speaker Nancy Pelosi, says in so many words: It's important to pass the bill now. We can read it later and find out what's in the bill. Is this the way our Congress carries out the will of the people? They don't even know what is in the laws they pass?

The best way our Congress could show they really respect the Constitution of this country and their own constituencies would be to enact legislation to limit senators and representatives to two consecutive terms in office.

And finally, we need to get away from the Washington scene

and the "Eastern Establishment." Why not move our Congress to somewhere in the middle of the country—St. Louis, perhaps?

GOVERNING BOARDS AND EDUCATIONAL INSTITUTIONS—THE ROOT OTHE PROBLEM?

It should be obvious by now that the primary problem in this country is at the top of two pyramids—governing boards of all types of organizations and universities and colleges.

I believe that governing boards should be using their expertise and backgrounds to question the whys and wherefores of their operations. My experiences and observations have led me to believe that most governing boards become subservient to the person they hire to run their organization. Men or women on these boards have a business, profession, or position that requires most of their attention.

As a result, they rely on the president, CEO, or whatever title is conferred on the head of the organization to provide them with information and suggestions as to the status and course(s) of action for their particular organization.

Why hadn't school boards taken note of the problems in education years ago? In many cities, only 50 percent of students make it through high school and graduate. In addition, those who do graduate are at the performance level of seventh graders twenty to fifty years ago. Why haven't school board members looked at these statistics and questioned the educators about how and why this is happening?

One reason may be found in where the teachers and media

people get their start—the universities and colleges of this country. These schools have been graduating students into the teaching and media fields who are not adequately prepared for their professions. Emphasis, at the collegiate level, has been placed on the sciences and traditionally classical fields, in terms of the salaries of the faculty and budgets of the departments.

These institutions of higher education have not looked at these two fields—education and media—as scholarly and important. Money and status have not been conferred on these two fields of study.

To me, entrance requirements for a college of education or media studies should be similar to the requirements for entrance into law schools and medical schools. Students should be required to have good grades in such courses as English, mathematics, history, geography, economics, political science, the humanities, and the sciences, such as chemistry and physics.

After four years and a bachelor's degree in what used to be called liberal arts, they would then be required to pass an entrance exam before acceptance into a college of education or whatever name is conferred on media studies. Let us face it: Teachers should be literate in all the above classes if they are going to be teaching school. I have heard many teachers and people in radio and television make gross errors in the English language—the use of "with he and I" is only one bad example.

It should be obvious that elementary and secondary school education today is failing. I mentioned earlier the statistics of the failure in performance of elementary and secondary students. Last year one major university I know of started a new remedial course for entering freshman students in mathematics. This was done because entering high school graduates did not meet the minimum level of expertise in order to take the college-level freshman course in mathematics.

Very little attention was paid to the announcement by the university of this change. The decision to impose this class requirement on all entering students should have been a warning about what has happened in our schools. As far as I could tell, very little notice or attention was paid by the media, and therefore the public, as to what this meant. We are graduating students from high school without the basic requirements for entrance into a university!

This says a lot about what has been happening in our elementary, junior high, and high schools. Have students just been passed along each year even if they didn't have the proper background in a course such as mathematics? Or, you could ask, do the teachers have the knowledge and ability from their college studies to be teaching such a subject at the high school level?

My contention is that many students are graduating from education colleges who are not proficient in many of the basic courses they may be asked to teach upon graduation. The same holds true for students graduating and going into the fields of print journalism, radio, and television. How can young people be expected to speak correct English when they continually hear people on radio or television say, incorrectly, "with he and I"? Have English teachers, under the guise that English is a "living language," said this is now proper English?

In the last sixty-five years this country has produced thousands, if not millions, of teachers. They, for the most part, have become highly unionized across the country and have strong political clout. Are most of them proficient in math, English, geography, and history? I hear teachers speak incorrect English—it's no wonder that many people do not speak or write correct English.

There is little hope of promotions or pay raises for teachers who might excel in their profession. This is because the union's seniority system will not allow for this. In effect, poorly performing teachers cannot be removed. This has occurred at the expense of those in the private sector.

Generous pay and benefits in the public sector have outpaced those of the private sector continuously. This happens even when the economy is flat or going down. This is dangerous when the citizens, meaning the taxpayers, cannot control expenditures within the available budget. However, we were warned about this danger as far back as 1937. And guess who warned us? It was none other than a Democrat, President Franklin Delano Roosevelt. The warning came in a letter to the National Federation of Federal Employees. Quoted verbatim below is a portion of the six-paragraph letter.

"Particularly, I want to emphasize my conviction that militant tactics have no place in the function of any organization of Government employees. Upon employees in the Federal Service rests the obligation to serve the whole people, whose interests and welfare requires orderliness and continuity in the conduct of Government activities. This obligation is paramount. Since their own services have to do with the functioning of the Government, strikes of public employees manifests nothing less than an intent on their part to prevent or obstruct the operations of Government until their demands are satisfied. Such action, looking toward the paralysis of Government by those who have sworn to support it, is unthinkable and intolerable."

Through the years since then, this was considered to mean all governments that relied on taxpayer monies. In 1955, AFL-CIO President George Meany said, "It is impossible to bargain collectively with the government." Now some governors have unilaterally issued edicts reversing this policy. These negotiations involve your tax money and you have nothing to say about it. Also to be considered is the fact that public service employee numbers have grown astronomically, so that today public service union members outnumber those union members working in the private sector.

Public sector employees, including such groups as teachers, police, and firefighters, have escalated their pay and benefits to a level way out of proportion to employees in the private sector. And it has come at a cost. President Roosevelt's warning was prophetic. Many cities and some states are near or at bankruptcy because there isn't enough tax money to cover the expenditures.

The negotiators in government, such as those in governing boards of all types and legislative bodies, have given in to the demands made by these public sector associations under the threat of possible strikes and work stoppage. As I am finishing this book, thousands of teachers in Chicago left hundreds of thousands of children without classes for over a week while they struck for about 20 percent more pay and benefits. We are supposed to forget the fact that their average pay of about $75,000 per year plus benefits may be one of the highest in the country. This comes while the economy has been in terrible shape, with one of the highest rates of unemployment in our history. Obviously the teachers' request for an increase cannot be based on their superior teaching performance. My understanding is that only 50 percent of their students make it through high school. And, as I wrote earlier, those who are graduating are at the performance level of seventh graders twenty to fifty years ago.

Let us turn now to the print and electronic media. Requirements for students majoring in print or broadcast journalism should be just as intensive as those for aspiring teachers. In addition to the how-to-do-it classes for a particular medium, I would put strong emphasis on such disciplines as English, political science, economics, American history, and speech. But all of this will not solve one of the major problems and criticisms you hear today. This is the criticism that many journalists are so liberal that the resulting product is biased since it is not balanced and therefore not objective.

Is this criticism fair? I say that it is. Most of the men and women being accused would violently object and defend their actions. Let's face it. Those people are not inherently bad people doing the wrong thing. So what is the truth about this situation and what causes it? To begin my answer, I want to go back to an incident I wrote about earlier. It's the incident of the noted Harvard professor who announced to the press that he had polled the entire Harvard faculty and found not a one who would vote for President Bush.

To me, it's obvious that the faculty is not balanced and that they are all thinking and leaning in the same direction when it comes to political questions or ideas. How can a faculty get to this position of thought with no consideration of both sides of an issue? A partial answer may be found in how faculty members are selected. Applying faculty members are reviewed and selected by the current faculty, which votes on the final selection. This sounds fair and correct, but is it?

It appears to be very democratic. In fact, it's pure democracy. Everybody gets to vote on everything. The Greeks didn't like this form and they abandoned it. This is why the founders of this country formed a republic with democratic principles in which the people vote through their representatives. Over a sixty-year period, this type of activity is apt to create a group mentality. The members of the group begin to think alike and act alike. Students then may not be exposed to other viewpoints on a variety of subjects. It's the only reason I can come up with to explain why so many people in print and electronic journalism are so openly biased in their reporting and interviewing.

It has been over thirty-five years since I retired as a professor, department head, and division director without a PhD degree. I had a master's degree in educational psychology. I started my academic career in 1955 when some people were still being hired and promoted for their work experience. I don't believe that is happening much anymore except maybe on the community college level.

I can't think of any other reason to account for so many journalists being so far to the left in their news coverage than the influence of their professors and also their teachers, who were prepared by these same professors. You might say that the Association of University Professors is a union with only select membership. Governing boards in higher education need to take a closer look at their schools. When athletic coaches are earning more than the presidents of these institutions and sports become the all-important item, then something has really gone wrong.

In earlier chapters I listed various problems that have developed because of the misunderstanding of the difference between Democracies and Republics. My spell checker, as I typed the last sentence, indicated an error in "democracies." I needed a capital D. It didn't correct the small R in "Republic."

I am not sure that boards controlling institutions of higher education know the changes that have occurred in their institutions in the last forty to sixty years. I know that years ago many individuals with master's degrees were given positions as department heads and even deans of colleges. The doctoral degree was not a requirement for the positions.

A typical example would be a mining executive of a major company becoming the dean of a mining college. People with work experience and status in the agricultural businesses would become deans or department heads of an agricultural college. People who were successful in drama and music and the arts would become department heads or deans without the PhD degree. My journalism professor and department head in the late '40s, who had been a newspaper editor, is another good example.

My own experience was in the newspaper, radio, and television businesses. With a master's degree I became a professor, a department head, and a division director. Apparently, in some disciplines where scholarly research might not be necessary, professional experience was accepted in higher education.

Today, the situation, generally, appears to be entirely different. The PhD degree has become a requirement. In effect, you have a union of people dictating how universities should be run—not the presidents, vice presidents, and governing boards. Why and how did this happen? I believe the why is answered by the how.

When I was a department head and division director, I filled vacancies on the basis of a person's resume, which included work experience and education, and a personal interview. All the faculty members had education and experience in radio and television. The faculty members taught one or two classes in their specialty and then assumed staff positions in the three broadcast stations as writers, producers, directors, and on-air personnel. It was an efficient arrangement and it created great rapport between faculty members and their students.

This, I learned later, was in contrast to what had been happening on campuses across the country. It turns out that faculty members on most campuses do the selection of new members. Applicants are interviewed by the entire faculty. It sounds and looks very democratic, doesn't it? It's a pure democracy—everybody gets to vote. The Greeks abandoned this system as a failure many centuries ago and our founding fathers didn't like it when they formed this country. As I wrote earlier, they formed a republic with democratic principles.

What might be the effect of this arrangement? I believe that the net effect of this is that faculties choose people who think like they think. That could mean social issues as well as political issues. Could this account for what I wrote earlier about the Harvard faculty? Remember, the vaunted faculty member proudly announced that he had polled the entire Harvard faculty and that not a single one would vote for President Bush.

I happen to feel that this type of recruitment and hiring of faculty has had a big effect on our educational systems. It has produced our teachers for the past sixty years and our print and electronic journalists in the same period of time. This has created such a brainwashing that most feel that the criticism leveled at them is unfair. They honestly believe that their coverage of the news is fair and balanced. And that is to be expected. From the time they started elementary school and up through college, they have been subjected to the party philosophy that doesn't leave room for balanced viewpoints. This is a serious problem in the fields of print and electronic journalism.

I have thought long and hard about this final part of the book, which shows how bad parts of the educational system have become. I have worried about it being self-serving because it relates to my own personal experience. But I have finally decided that it's important enough to show how bad things can happen at an institution of higher education.

After nearly twenty-five years at the University of Arizona, my wife of twenty-five years died after a lengthy illness. The vice president to whom I reported, Marvin D. Johnson, suggested I take advantage of an opportunity for a sabbatical that had become available at the University of Texas. I should add that Mr. Johnson was very popular and highly regarded by many alumni throughout the country. I learned from a source who attended the meeting where a decision was to be made that another vice president, who had a PhD, objected to Johnson's nomination to become president because he only had a master's degree and was not faculty. Johnson didn't receive the appointment.

I was in Texas when Vice President Johnson resigned to assume a vice presidential position at the University of New Mexico. He later went on to become a vice president of a major corporation in Colorado. When Johnson left, the new Arizona president called me in Texas to tell me about the move and of a temporary replacement, to whom I would be reporting.

On my return to Tucson from the sabbatical, I learned that virtually everyone in a staff capacity who used to report to Vice President Johnson had been removed. I was the only one remaining, probably because of my faculty status. I went to pay my respects to Johnson's temporary replacement. Almost immediately, I heard the following comment: "Well, Frank, I've heard how great you are. I guess we'll have a year to find out, won't we?" Immediately, I went to see the president.

I told him I had another job offer that I hadn't planned to take but that I didn't like what I was seeing and hearing about my position. He told me how much he valued my work and urged me to stay. On the basis of what I was told, I decided to stay and tuned down the other offer.

Some months later, I was out of town attending a PBS Board of Directors meeting. When I returned, I learned that the vice president who had stopped Johnson's appointment to the presidency had had a meeting with my faculty and staff to announce that my area was being broken up into three units and that there would be three individuals replacing me. Obviously, they turned out to be people with PhD degrees.

I again went to see the president to see how this could be happening after he had urged me to stay. The answer I received from an individual who couldn't even look at me eye to eye while saying it was: "Frank, I have two other people reporting to me and I can't come between you!"

Naturally, I couldn't believe what I had just heard and I left in disgust. I decided not to stay and become bitter in my old age, so I took early retirement even though I lost some of my retirement pay. But I couldn't be happier with my decision to get out when I did. With my new wife, I started a new career. While I was putting together our own commercial FM radio station, my wife, Gail, was opening and running our new travel agency and tour company.

As I wrote earlier, I wasn't sure the book should end with these last series of events. But I have decided that it's an example of some of the things that go on at the collegiate level of education. There is little responsibility and accountability. The emphasis on the PhD has become a union card. There is no way to get rid of bad teachers because of the tenure system.

Finally, the impact of how students are taught from the first grade through college will continue to have a profound effect on our country now and into the future.

EPILOGUE: WAKE UP AMERICA

I thought I finished this book with the last chapter. However, events that took place since then have compelled me to write this epilogue.

What are these events? They are the upcoming inauguration of our current president, the misinformation relating to the controversy about gun ownership in this country, the financial status of this nation's economy—which is no different now than it was four years ago—and the roles of journalism in our society today.

My wife suggested a title for this book which I did not use. However, I now choose it as a theme and title for this epilogue: "Wake up America."

It is very hard to wake up the American public when so many members of the national press give every appearance that they are an arm of the national government in Washington. This is especially true of the office of the president. Unfortunately most of these members of the press think they are doing a fair and objective job. There seems to be little or no investigative reporting. Presidential press conferences are a laugh. No one can ask follow-up questions, if they are allowed. They don't appear to check on items to see if they are true. They listen to the president's prepared remarks and accept practically everything that is said as gospel.

The most glaring example of this is the terrorist attack in Libya just before the last presidential election. In this case, terrorists attacked an American consulate, considered US territory in a foreign country, and killed the ambassador and three other US citizens. All of this was done by Islamic terrorists. If you watched television or listened to the radio, you wouldn't know this was happening. Most of the media ignored the story.

This happened at the consular property in Benghazi, just a short distance from the embassy in Tripoli. The ambassador's office warned Washington officials that a dangerous situation was developing and they asked for help. Just previous to this incident, the British recalled their ambassador because of a shooting incident. The ambassador's requests apparently went unheeded. Was this because the incident occurred right before the election? After all, part of the president's campaign was that Islamic terrorism was on the decline. He used the killing of bin Laden to reinforce that assumption. Was a terrorist raid on American property and the killing of four US citizens considered bad news for the president's reelection campaign? Furthermore, I assume that an incident of this magnitude would bring all of our top officials, including the president, into the situation room to monitor the events taking place and to take an appropriate response to save the lives of our citizens.

When the lame explanation came out that an obscure and little-known film had caused the local disturbance, where were the highly touted news people questioning this story? Where was the investigative reporting to get the facts? We had the necessary forces at the naval air station at Sigonella, Sicily. They might have saved the situation and the lives of our citizens. But they were never ordered into action. I can't understand why the news media weren't all over this story.

Let us now turn to a domestic situation in which the press apparently dropped the ball. The president made many promises during his first election campaign. One was that he had the answers to fixing the serious unemployment situation which was and is badly hurting the economy. He said he would fix that and bring prosperity back to this country. In his second campaign for reelection, I didn't see or hear reporters questioning him about the fact that unemployment in the country is at about the same level or even a little higher than four years ago. The criticism that the press, in general, supports the president and is reluctant to report on anything that might detract from his popularity appears to have some validity. Are they really so liberal that they can't bring themselves to be fair, impartial, and objective in their news coverage?

Finally, I do want to write about the gun controversy. First I want to present the Second Amendment to our Constitution. This is one of nine amendments proposed by the same people who wrote and approved the original constitution. The amendments were proposed in 1779 and then approved in 1791. They are considered our Bill of Rights. They are the rights granted to all citizens by our Constitution. They were presented and approved by the people who founded this republic of ours. The Second Amendment reads: "A well-regulated Militia, being necessary to the security of a free State, the right of the people to keep and bear Arms, shall not be infringed."

Some of the amendments included in the Bill of Rights are: freedom of religion, property rights, the restriction on double jeopardy, the right to be free from unreasonable search and seizure, the right to a speedy trial, rights to a trial by a jury of our peers, no cruel and unusual punishment, and the stipulations that the amendments shall not be construed to be the only rights retained by the people and the powers not delegated to the national governments are reserved to the individual states. All of these amendments provide a basis for our freedoms in this country. It may be interesting to note that the first two amendments that seem to indicate the priorities of the founding fathers were freedom of religion and gun ownership.

With regard to the Second Amendment, I do not see too many members of the press learning about and explaining to the public what constitutes an "assault" weapon in terms of firearms. Because of bad press reporting or politicians talking about things without knowing the facts, there may be a perception that the Bushmaster AR-15 Rifle is an assault weapon. It is no such thing. People who want to control guns use the word "assault" as a scare tactic.

Rifles, originally, were single-shot. Once you fired, you pulled back the bolt, which ejected the empty cartridge casing. Then you pushed the bolt forward to place another bullet in the chamber, ready to fire. Each time you fired you used the bolt action and then you again pulled the trigger to fire the weapon. The bullets are in cartridges of various sizes. They are spring loaded to keep pushing the next bullet up toward the firing chamber of the rifle.

The next development was the semi-automatic rifle. Instead of pulling and then pushing the bolt, the firing of the bullet itself expels the shell casing and another bullet is put into the chamber, ready to fire. Therefore, you have to pull the trigger each time you want to fire, the same as you do in a single-shot rifle. Most handguns operate on the same principle. This is the way many hunting rifles fire and is also the system for the AR-15. It's a former military rifle, where you pull the trigger each time you fire. This is called a semi-automatic. You can see why the people pushing for gun controls want to call it an assault rifle. This sounds more dangerous than if you call it a semi-automatic rifle. This type of rifle is commonly used in hunting and on target ranges.

The next stage is the automatic, where you pull the trigger

and can hold it to empty the entire magazine, if you wish. And, of course, you call this a machine gun. Personally, I do not call the AR-15 an assault rifle just because it was used at one time many years ago in the military.

Now, let's get back to the Second Amendment. It reads "The right of the people to keep and bear arms shall not be infringed." The founders also reserved all rights to the individual states except those specifically assigned to the national government.

These people saw what a strong centralized government could do to individual freedoms. They separated the powers among three branches—Congressional, Judicial, and Presidential. The power, in most cases, rests with the Congress—House and Senate—with the Congress representing the will of the people. At this time we have the presidential branch trying to centralize control. This is what the founding fathers feared. It is the start toward socialism and then totalitarianism.

However, the Congress is not without criticism. To truly represent the people's interests, the Congress should not make decisions on the basis of getting reelected. They would do a much better job on our behalf if they had the same limitation of two consecutive terms that they had imposed on the office of the president many years ago. We definitely need fresh blood in office every two terms to really do justice to the rights and opinions of the citizens of this country.

These framers of our Declaration of Independence and the Constitution and its Bill of Rights wanted to make sure that we did not allow a national government to ever become like the one with which they had just fought for independence.

This is the real danger we face today. WAKE UP AMERICA!

Printed in the USA
CPSIA information can be obtained
at www.ICGtesting.com
LVHW040313250124
769870LV00029B/60